Reading Together

WALKING THROUGH THE JUNGLE

Read it together

Walking Through the Jungle takes children on an adventure where they become explorers in a colourful jungle, meeting one wild animal after another.

The strong pattern of the story, with a question on each page, helps children take a very active part in the book.

The story introduces children to lots of words which invite them to play with the way language sounds.

Leaping through the jungle
What do you see?
Can you hear a noise?
ROAR!
What could it be?

Is it a lion?

I like it when the crocodile snap snaps with his big teeth!

The catchy rhyme and rhythm help children to remember the story and encourage them to join in. Leave them spaces to say the parts of the story they know.

Because it's so easily remembered, children will be able to tell you the story quite quickly, using some words from the book and some of their own.

Can you hear a noise?
What could it be?
Over there! ...

A monkey looking for his tea.

Children might decide to act out the story with their toys or a friend. It's a really good way for them to get to know it and helps to build their confidence with books.

Where's my tea?
I'm a very, very hungry lion.

umping through the jungle,
What can I see?
I can hear a noise ...
It's a lion!

We hope you enjoy reading this book together.

First published 1993 by Walker Books Ltd
87 Vauxhall Walk, London SE11 5HJ

This edition published 2005

2 4 6 8 10 9 7 5 3 1

Printed in China

ISBN 1-4063-0061-6

www.walkerbooks.co.uk

WALKING THROUGH THE JUNGLE

Illustrated by
Julie Lacome

WALKER BOOKS
AND SUBSIDIARIES
LONDON · BOSTON · SYDNEY · AUCKLAND

Walking through the jungle,
What do you see?
Can you hear a noise?
What could it be?

SSSsss

Over there!
A snake
looking
for his tea.

Leaping through the jungle,
What do you see?
Can you hear a noise?
What could it be?

roarrrr

Over there!
A lion
looking
for his tea.

Running through the jungle,
What do you see?
Can you hear a noise?
What could it be?

trump trump

Over there!
An elephant
looking
for his tea.

Swinging through the jungle,
What do you see?
Can you hear a noise?
What could it be?

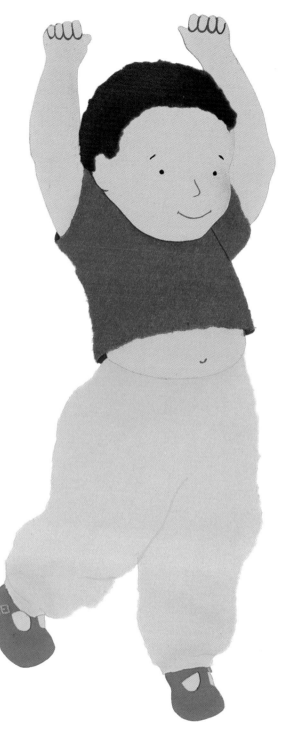

chitter chatter

Over there!
A monkey
looking
for his tea.

Wading through the jungle,
What do you see?
Can you hear a noise?
What could it be?

snap snap

Over there!
A crocodile
looking
for his tea ...

Hope it isn't

me!

Read it again

It's an ... elephant!

Guess the animal

As you read aloud, your child can take part in the story by making the animal sounds. Slowly slide back the page to help them guess the animal hiding beneath which is making the terrible

SSSsss roarrrrr trump

Swing like a monkey

You can help children bring the story alive by encouraging them to act out the different animal movements: leaping like a lion, running like an elephant, swinging like a monkey.

With your help, they could also make up another story using a different set of animals:
Hopping through the garden…
Swimming through
the blue sea…

Leaping like a lion

Running like an elephant

Find the animal

You could play "find the animal" games where children search through the book looking for the animal that roars; the animal with tusks; the parrot; the animals with tails; or those with four legs, two legs or … no legs!

It's the crocodile that snaps!

Make a picture
Making a collage picture of a favourite animal using magazines, tissue and wrapping paper is an enjoyable way of imitating the beautiful illustrations in this book.

Tell a story
Children can use animal toys to retell the story in their own words. They can use the pictures in the book to help them, perhaps adding sound effects. They could beat out the rhythm of the story using a tray, tambourine, or any musical toy.

Swinging like a monkey